PABLO PICASSO

PICASSO

John Galloway

Chairman, Department of Art
Oakland University

McGRAW-HILL BOOK COMPANY · NEW YORK · LONDON · TORONTO · SYDNEY

Cover picture, *A Mother Holding a Child and Four Studies of her Right Hand* (1904), crayon drawing, courtesy of the Fogg Art Museum, Harvard University, bequest of Meta and Paul J. Sachs. Photograph for Frontispiece, courtesy John D. Schiff. Photograph for Figure 1, courtesy MAS Reproducciones. Photograph for Figure 4, courtesy Geoffrey Clements Photography. Photographs for Figures 16 and 20, courtesy Service de Documentation Photographique de la Réunion des Musées Nationaux.

FEW ARTISTS have equalled Picasso's impact upon our way of seeing. The visual wealth of his art, a major reality of twentieth-century perception, reaches us both in its own thrust and through its influence upon two generations of painters and sculptors. Picasso's leadership as both pioneer and activist of modern art is indisputable. His founding of Cubism, the first style of this century to break radically with the past, and his relentless development of that style in the face of critical abuse, removed barriers which might well have blocked acceptance of more recent movements.

Although great controversy has marked Picasso's career, today neither his admirers nor his assailants any longer call him revolutionary. More recent developments in the fine arts have supplanted the once explosive shock of his Cubist discoveries and many of today's young skeptics have forgotten or have not learned that the innovations of Cubism in the second decade of this century were met by almost universal hostility. Certain of his supporters lament Picasso's continual adherence to themes rooted in visual reality instead of creating totally abstract form. Others who applauded him for five decades now feel that he has permitted himself to be institutionalized by sycophants, particularly since the close of World War II, and has since failed to produce masterpieces as startling as his earlier works. But no later art, from Kandinsky's brilliant early abstractions to Futurism, Dada, *de Stijl,* and recent Pop or Op and Minimal trends, has more stridently challenged us than did Cubism.

Like other masters in the history of art, Picasso became an iconoclast only after he had fully grasped the accepted styles he eventually displaced. Although he always honored his source of inspiration, he regarded each influence as an entity to be learned and respected but superseded.

He was born Pablo Ruiz Picasso on October 25, 1881, in Málaga on Spain's Andalusian coast. His father, an ill-paid art teacher, encouraged him to become a painter and was his first instructor. After living in La Coruña for a few years, the family moved in 1895 to Barcelona where Picasso, at age fourteen, won admittance to advanced classes at the School of Fine Arts. He finished in one day the examinations for which a month was allowed. His canvas *Science and Charity,* with its Munch-like theme of a sickroom and visiting doctor, won honorable mention at the Madrid national exhibition of 1897. Now sixteen, Picasso passed with distinction the entrance requirements of the conservative Royal Academy in Madrid; but he withdrew in the spring of 1898, nominally because of a scarlet fever attack though chiefly out of boredom with the pedantic instruction which he so easily mastered.

Picasso returned to Barcelona late in 1898 after convalescing from the fever and then painting from nature in Horta de Ebro. Joining the self-styled "Barbarians" of Catalonian bohemia at the café called *Els Quatre Gats* (The Four Cats), he enjoyed the most stimulating intellectual experience offered by Spain at that time. The *Quatre Gats* rebels confronted him with a mélange of current arts and letters: *Art Nouveau,* Pre-Raphaelitism, Aubrey Beardsley, Oscar Wilde, Nietzschean philosophy and Wagnerian music, Ibsen and other Scandinavian writers, and possibly Edvard Munch's paintings or graphics, and, among other French poets and critics, the Symbolists Rimbaud, Baudelaire, and Verlaine.

Picasso's growth was phenomenal in his formative years, but most of his early artistic influences stemmed from northern European rather than Spanish sources. Antonio Gaudí, already celebrated in Barcelona for his *modernista* architecture, did not strongly affect Picasso's aesthetic. In fact, few Spanish contemporaries appealed to him except for the artist Isidro Nonell (1873-1911) and the poet Jaime Sabartés (1881-1968). Nonell's paintings of the poor soon influenced the young Spaniard's style as well as his choice of subjects, and Sabartés became his lifelong friend and biographer.

It is not surprising that the young Picasso's drawings and paintings of the late 1890's (Figure 1) reveal the effects of contemporary French art, for Paris at the turn of the century was summoning intellectuals and artists from America and from all parts of Europe. At age nineteen Picasso was impatient to explore at first hand the cultural wealth he knew largely through foreign journals and reproductions. Although he was grateful for the impetus he had received from the group at *Els Quatre Gats,* and enjoyed drawing for the *modernista* review *Joventut,* he doubted that Barcelona, even at its best, could satisfy his ambitions and intellectual curiosity. So in October, 1900, depleting the meager savings of his family, Picasso made his first visit to Paris, where he revelled in the great museum collections and exhibitions of contemporary painting and sculpture.

Picasso returned to Spain each year between 1901 and 1904, once attempting to animate Madrid's lagging intellectual circle by serving as art editor of the journal *Arte Joven* (*Young Art*); but again the cultural environment of his own country disappointed him. The challenge of Paris drew him there permanently in April, 1904.

The search for a viable style during the four years of transition from Spain to the French capital brought Picasso closer than ever to the arabesques and interior lighting of works by Toulouse-Lautrec, Vuillard, Bonnard, and Manet. Degas' deft, elegant line and shimmering brushwork also provided instruction. The influence of these artists is evident in such early paintings as *Portrait of a Woman* (Slide 1), but already the young Spaniard's own vivacity is clearly felt.

During the summer of 1901 Picasso's independence increased and his first distinctively personal style, the renowned Blue Period, emerged in autumn of that year. This manner, which dominated his painting until late 1904, couples a fragile melancholy of line and blue tonality with somber figures and settings (Slide 2). Many authorities on Picasso's stylistic development

Figure 1.
The Artist's Sister (1899)
charcoal and pastel
Museo Picasso, Barcelona

have not emphasized the relevance of the Blue Period to the development of Cubism—perhaps because there are few obvious similarities between individual pictures from these two styles. However, it was at this time that Picasso discovered a concept which has since remained central to his art: if the theme or subject of a picture is to be stressed, it must be conveyed chiefly through formal means; conversely, if conceptual qualities are to dominate, the subject matter must be adjusted accordingly. In sum, Picasso learned during the Blue Period that theme and style must be harmonized to achieve the fullest expressive impact. An awareness of his studied relationship of subject matter with the factors of line, shape, space, texture, and tone and their specific conveyance of mood, is indispensable to our understanding of the Blue Period and its relation to Picasso's subsequent development.

Picasso's preference for the color blue, attenuated and sometimes emaciated figures, linear emphases of restrained body gestures, and themes of loneliness and even withdrawal, may be traced to many sources in literature and art, as well as to his own precarious economic and professional status from 1901 until late 1904. Symbolist poetry; writings of the Decadents; Gauguin's and Maurice Denis' aesthetic theories; Nonell's paintings and Théophile Steinlen's journal illustrations of the poor; and the distortions of the Spanish Mannerists El Greco and Morales have also been frequently ascribed as sources for the Blue Period melancholy.

Picasso's canvases of this formative stage speak, however, with a hushed eloquence which is singularly his own. In fact, many of these "influences" did not strongly affect him until after he had begun to form the substance of the Blue Period style. It has been almost invariably true that Picasso's discoveries of inspiring stimuli have corresponded to trends already existent in his own art and have confirmed rather than caused his direction.

The thin proportions and strained postures of the Blue Period subjects do reflect some kinship with Nonell's style and perhaps with El Greco's, but it is more likely that the type was actually taken from outcasts Picasso saw in the poverty-stricken sections of Barcelona and Madrid, where blind beggars, for example, were notably common; and the cheap cafés and destitute drunkards of Montmartre also provided spectacles of degradation. These slumped, hollow individuals existed within Picasso's sight and required little art historical or literary confirmation, although he may have consciously added the poignancy of Nonell, El Greco, and possibly Van Gogh to his own.

The gauntness of most of the Blue Period figures contributes to the prevalent somberness, yet many of the nude or thinly draped women also reveal a fragile sensuousness (Slide 3). Although their setting is preeminently bluish, even at the height of this style in 1903 Picasso minimized the omnipresence of blue by subtly introducing warm whites and faint pinks in the flesh or garments of the figures.

Blue is a color which Picasso has always especially loved independently of its possible symbolic attributes. He has flooded with blue many later pictures which range in expression from frivolity to claustrophobia. Blue, of itself, is not necessarily saddening in effect; it may be vivacious, or it may be depressing. Experiments in facsimile compositions in which sulphurous or acid yellows and muddy reds replace the blues of the 1901-1904 works have

shown that equal, if not more intense, states of sadness are yielded by tones other than blue. Also, many observers find the bleak immediacy of such canvases as *Man and Woman* (Figure 2) as penetrating in black and white reproduction as in the original colors; and certainly one of the most gripping of all Blue Period works is *The Frugal Repast* of 1904, not a painting but a black and white etching.

The transition from the Blue Period to the Rose Period of 1905-1906 began late in 1904, after Picasso had moved into the ramshackle structure in Montmartre which Max Jacob christened the "Bateau-Lavoir" (Boat Laundry). This untidy shelter, with little plumbing and no heat, was a haven nonetheless for Picasso and the several avant-garde artists who lived or visited there.

To some extent the Rose Period was probably due to encouraging developments in Picasso's personal life and professional career. The preceding four years had begun without warm prospect for the young Spaniard who did not yet speak French, but who still determinedly sought his way in Parisian bohemia. During 1901 and 1902 he had associated in Paris chiefly with fellow Spaniards such as the artists Sebastian Junyer, Manolo Hugué, and Ricardo Canals, but through them and his first dealers, Berthe Weill and Ambroise Vollard, he gradually began to meet the brilliant young poets and painters who later stimulated and supported him. Even before he permanently settled in Paris in April, 1904 (the final year of the Blue Period), Picasso had begun to acquire a certain following. The poet Max Jacob encouraged him; Berthe Weill had sold a few of his pictures; his first one-man show with Vollard in 1901 though attracting little attention was praised by one critic, Félicien Fagus, who referred to Picasso's brilliant virility; and a Spanish businessman, Petrus Mañach, for a time regularly purchased, if at remarkably low prices, his generally neglected works.

The somber expressiveness of the Blue Period canvases gradually yielded to a new warmth, although the older, gaunt figures sometimes emerged through the beige and pink tones of the early Rose Period, also called the Circus Period (Slide 4 and Figure 3). But the thinness of the Rose Period actors, harlequins, jugglers, and acrobats now signifies the wiriness of circus professionals whose success depends so greatly upon perfectly timed movement. Sinuousness replaces fragility as more optimistic or tender poses and tonalities supplant the melancholy ones of the earlier style. Frequenting the Médrano Circus near the Place Pigalle, a more confident Picasso found instruction as well as entertainment in the supple forms and actions of the performers. A visit to Holland in the summer of 1905 provided him with an unfamiliar, flat landscape, and the full shapes of young Dutchwomen he saw there contributed to his new concern with weight and volume (Slide 5).

Picasso's environment during 1905 also embraced the magnificent collections of preclassical and classical arts, particularly sculptured reliefs and vases, at the Louvre. Assyrian, Egyptian, and possibly pre-Columbian Mayan carved panels must have influenced the pose, perhaps even the specific gestures of his figure paintings such as the remarkably dignified *Girl with a Fan* (Figure 4). Warmer blues than those of his preceding manner, warm grays, beige, a variety of

Figure 3.
The Actor (1905)
oil on canvas
76⅜″ x 44⅛″
Metropolitan Museum of Art
New York
Gift of Thelma Chrysler Foy
1952

pink tones, and delicate lavender passages are now prevalent and are sometimes heightened by accents of pure red.

Picasso, who had continued his friendship with the Spanish comrades of Blue Period days and with Max Jacob, now won the admiration of a small international circle which included the French writers André Salmon, Maurice Raynal, Guillaume Apollinaire, and Pierre Reverdy; the American writer Gertrude Stein and her brother Leo, both early collectors of Blue and Rose Period works; the Russian Sergei Shchukin, another enterprising purchaser; and the dealers Clovis Sagot and Daniel-Henry Kahnweiler. Before the end of the Rose Period, Picasso became acquainted with his fellow Spaniard, the painter Juan Gris, and with the Fauves Henri Matisse, André Derain, and slightly later, Georges Braque. Also around this time Picasso found special confidence in his love for Fernande Olivier, who was his model and companion.

The Rose Period, and the warmth of encouragement which attended it, amplified Picasso's aims as well as bringing to his pictures a warmer tonality and happier iconography. His study of the potentials of spatial structure and the search for essences of visual form led him swiftly during 1906 toward Cubism. A sub-phase which has been called the Classical Period just preceded Picasso's discovery of Spain's blunt Iberian classical art and of the bold formal synthesis of African sculpture, examples of which he already knew from the collections of Matisse and other Fauves. The structural lessons of these various sources appear in such paintings as the *Inclined Woman's Head* (Figure 5) and the celebrated *Portrait of Gertrude Stein* (Slide 6) of 1906. These show his new attention to the problems of relating a three-dimensional form to the flat picture plane and of reducing the details of an image to a strong pictorial synthesis. The appealing decorative qualities of sinuous line and delicate patterns of his Circus phase give way to blunter interpretations of shape and mass (Figure 6). Powerful simplifications of planes and shape appear in the *Self-Portrait* (Figure 7) which he painted in the autumn of 1906 when he also completed, after eighty sittings, the Gertrude Stein likeness. Rhythmic plays of light and dark relationships, as in the extension of the pattern at the hip and hand to the palette and across its upper edge, display his growing power to emphasize major thrusts and still resolve them within the plane of the composition itself.

At the end of the Rose Period in late 1906, Picasso, now twenty-five, had more than begun to prove himself. He knew that his Blue and Rose Period works had convinced a small but keenly selective group that he was a significant young artist. But his achievement and the discovery of exciting challenges in the formal structure of a new kind of art served only to make him restless.

Before 1907 Picasso's paintings typically directed the observer's attention to their evident or implicit narrative as much as to the color, space, line, and shape. Even his avant-garde admirers responded to the easily discerned elements of skill in the Rose Period canvases. But the raw, shocking imagery of the first great example of Cubism, *Les Demoiselles d'Avignon*

Figure 4.
Girl with a Fan (1905)
oil on canvas, 39″ x 31½″
Collection of the Honorable
and Mrs. W. Averell Harriman

13

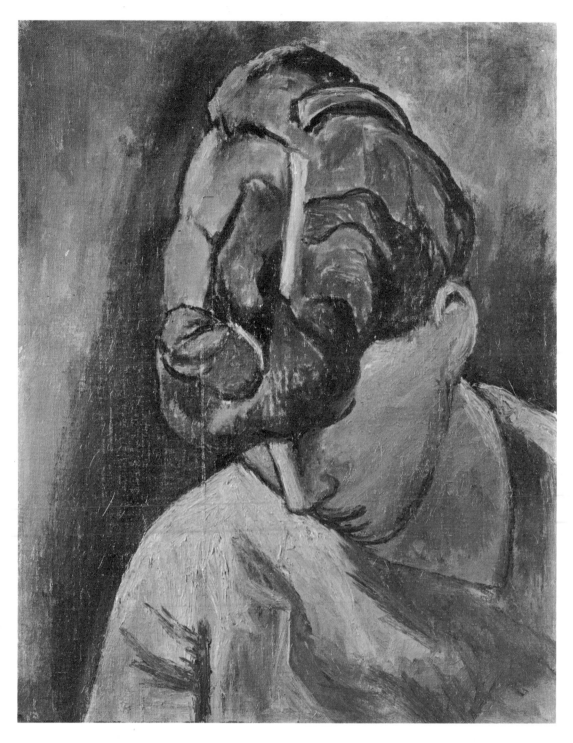

Figure 5.
Inclined Woman's Head (1906)
oil on canvas, 20″ x 12⅝″
Staatsgalerie, Stuttgart

Figure 6.
Woman with Loaves (1906)
oil on canvas, 39″ x 27½″
Philadelphia Museum of Art

(Figure 8), bewildered almost every one of Picasso's friends. Matisse, whose Fauvist pictures had recently been attacked by critics and the public as savage and incomprehensible, was troubled by the *Demoiselles,* and Braque and Derain were skeptical. Only Kahnweiler, now Picasso's dealer, was quick to perceive the revolutionary import of the splintered planes and grotesque shapes of the huge, eight-foot-square canvas. Most of the visitors to Picasso's studio, however, soon realized their initial failure to grasp the historical and aesthetic importance of this major landmark of early Cubist style. Its impact was so powerful that it became an art historical legend among Parisian painters even though it was not publicly exhibited until the 1930's.

Although this monument of early Cubism at first startled Picasso's most sophisticated admirers, the scores of drawings and paintings which preceded and followed it (Slides 7, 8 and 9) show a definite continuity. But so rapid was Picasso's stylistic development at this stage that, as in the *Demoiselles* itself, he sometimes even changed his manner within a particular composition.

At the outset the allegory of *Les Demoiselles d'Avignon* involved the visit of a sailor to a brothel on the Carrer d'Avinyo (Avignon Street) in Barcelona. As Picasso's exploration of planes and volumes grew more intense, the subject underwent changes; the sailor disappeared as did images of lesser significance in the jagged rhythms and spatial tensions of the composition itself. The forms of the five women disclose Picasso's excited response to African tribal carvings, especially those of the Ivory Coast and Gabon; and other influences, among them Spanish (Iberian) classical sculpture and medieval painting, are implicit.

The structural method of the great French Post-Impressionist master Cézanne is certainly one of the forces behind the *Demoiselles.* Cézanne, working in solitude late in his life and neglected by all but a very few admirers, had arrived at a powerful synthesis of spatial depth and three-dimensional form with the flat character of the picture plane. Although Picasso could not have seen a massive exhibition of Cézanne's canvases until the first Cézanne retrospective at the Salon d'Automne of 1907, one year after the master's death, he had certainly seen examples of the method which was to affect the aesthetic of all the artists who became Cubists.

In late 1907 or early 1908 Georges Braque, who had left the Fauves, joined Picasso to explore Cubist methods. Braque had found explicit guidance in Cézanne's still lifes, and Picasso, whose proper inspiration usually issued from the human figure, sometimes used the still life with acute skill in the play of bold and subtle contrasts of shape and light-to-dark tonalities (Slide 7). As if to modify the startling innovations of his gradually flattening space and distortion of form, Picasso chose restrained colors, especially muted greens, blues, tans, and a myriad of grays; in fact, tones similar to those used by Cézanne during his search for a new structural method. An increasingly vertical ordering of design is also characteristic of the 1908-1909 works.

The *Head of a Woman* of 1909 (Figure 9) is the first landmark of Cubist sculpture just as *Les Demoiselles d'Avignon* of 1907 had been the two-dimensional prototype of Cubist style.

Figure 7.
Self-Portrait (1906)
oil on canvas, 36″ x 28″
Philadelphia Museum of Art
A. E. Gallatin Collection

Figure 8.
Les Demoiselles d'Avignon (1907)
oil on canvas, 96″ x 92″
Museum of Modern Art, New York
Acquired through the Lillie P. Bliss Bequest

Figure 9.
Woman's Head (1909)
bronze, height 16¼″
Museum of Modern Art, New York

With vigorous planes and concavities Picasso here applies his Cubist principles to solid form. Sculpture has always commanded Picasso's study. In Barcelona he had worked in sculpture and we have seen that African and Iberian sculpture stimulated changes in his painting. However, the *Head of a Woman* is the only large modeled Cubist sculpture and the last sculpture in the round which Picasso made for twenty years. Instead, he turned to shaping Cubist constructions of unconventional materials which are the basis of much contemporary sculpture in that the form is constructed or built instead of modeled.

Although we use geometrical terms—plane, convexity, cube, cone, arc, for example—when we discuss Cubism, we should not confuse the aesthetic process of Picasso and Braque with a precise geometrical analysis. The name of the style, derisively coined by the critic Louis Vauxcelles in 1908 (or, perhaps by Matisse) is based upon an inexact study of the forms really used in Cubist paintings. While Picasso and Braque defiantly picked up the invective and began to call themselves Cubists, in actuality they did not break form into three-dimensional "little cubes" as Vauxcelles misguidedly claimed, but instead manipulated faceted or slightly hollowed surfaces of their subjects so that we see the same form in many positions in space (Figure 10).

By 1909 when Picasso moved from the once-provocative, encouraging atmosphere of the Bateau-Lavoir to a more comfortable studio-apartment at 11 Boulevard de Clichy, the advent of Cubism, especially the verbal fame of *Les Demoiselles d'Avignon,* had already reached widely into avant-garde circles in other European countries and America. Picasso, who seldom participated in the controversial Cubist group exhibitions in Paris, was given a one-man show

in 1909 in Munich. Although his work was still violently attacked by most of the public and press, he now won many visitors, admiring or curious, and his need for seclusion replaced the earlier impulse to converse with numbers of companions. Still living with the attractive and lively Fernande, and installed in a well-furnished studio, he began to be more selective in his acquaintances as his creative vision gained greater independence.

The period of late 1909 until late 1911 witnessed Picasso's and Braque's development of Analytic Cubism, a phase of the Cubist style which was anticipated by the bronze *Woman's Head* (Figure 9) and the *Seated Nude* (Figure 10). Analytic Cubist paintings develop even further the revolutionary concept of simultaneity which allows multiple aspects of the same form to be represented at the same instant in time and space. In other words, Picasso simultaneously shows us the side, quarter, and sometimes rear views, as well as the customary front and profile images, as though the spectator were moving around the object.

Analytic Cubism intensively reduced the forms of still life objects and the figure (Slide 9, Figure 11); specific identities became increasingly obscure as fragmented, interpenetrating arcs, planes, and purposive distortions of shape brought a complex resolution between form in space and the two-dimensional picture surface.

Cézanne's method was thus taken radically further. But neither Picasso nor Braque became altogether conceptual in theory or effect. Although Picasso's Analytic works are relatively more nearly abstract than those of the Blue and Rose Periods, they are, in fact, the result of a far more searching study of their subjects. Cubism, except at the hands of a very few of its advocates—Robert Delaunay and Marcel Duchamp, for example—was not the vehicle of abstraction. However distantly, the underlying form and significance and the specific image of Picasso's subject emerged in the Analytic paintings. Rightly or wrongly, Picasso has maintained "There is no abstract art. You must always start with something. Afterward you can remove all traces of reality, [but] the idea of the object will have left an indelible mark." *(The Art of Painting in the Twentieth Century,* edited by Pierre Seghers and Jacques Charpier, Hawthorn, 1965).

The years 1911 and 1912, in which Picasso explored one possibility of pictorial analysis after another, also brought eventual changes of environment and recognition. Alfred Stieglitz's "Photo-Secession" Gallery in New York presented a one-man show of his work; Kahnweiler published a book by the poet Max Jacob illustrated by Picasso's etchings; he moved back to Montparnasse, and now, leaving Fernande, fell in love with Marcelle Humbert (called "Eva" by Picasso); and, at age thirty, he already enjoyed international prestige among vanguard artists. The Italian Futurists, whose style owed much to the Cubist aesthetic, visited him in Paris; and the sensitive English critic Roger Fry actively supported his art in London, where in 1912 Picasso's drawings were given a one-man exhibition at the Stafford Gallery.

The year 1912 also brought Synthetic Cubism, a phase which had been anticipated by both Picasso's and Braque's collage or *papier collé* techniques of the winter of 1911 when they first began to mount paper cut-outs, linoleum, wallpaper patterns, and corrugated pasteboard into

Figure 10.
Seated Nude (1909)
oil on canvas, 36¼″ x 28¾″
Tate Gallery, London

21

Figure 11.
*Portrait of
Daniel-Henry Kahnweiler*
(1910)
oil on canvas
39⅝" x 28⅝"
Art Institute of Chicago
Gift of
Mrs. Gilbert W. Chapman

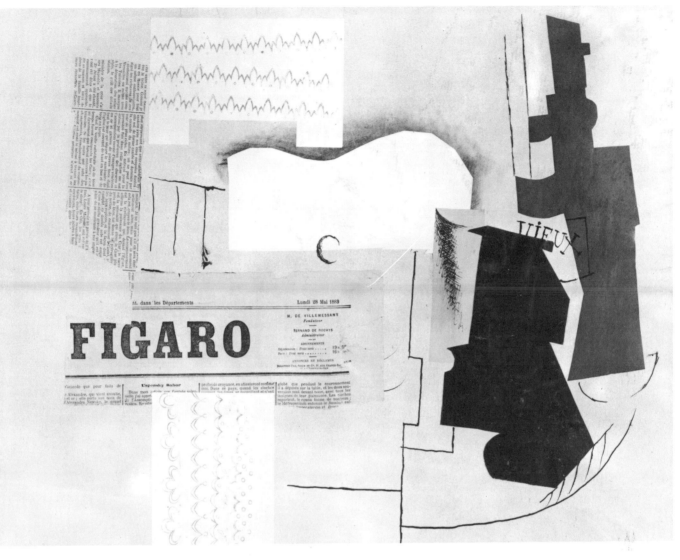

apparently random, but actually firmly ordered, compositions on the picture surface (Slide 10, Figure 12). Following their example, the other Cubists, now a score of artists who ardently discussed theory and the practical matters of exhibiting, were soon including in their canvases fragments of their daily environment of the studio and night café: bits of journals in which their art was reviewed, stringed instruments, the virile textures of wood-graining and sand-roughened pigment or blurred charcoal line.

The Synthetic collages mark a notable departure from the Analytic approach, yet they incorporate rather than reject the older aesthetic. Their general effect is one of fewer pictorial elements, greater textural variety and openness of design, and flatter, more liberated space. Where the Analytic Cubist works apparently attempted to "analyze" the inner structure of a given object by viewing it simultaneously from different aspects, the new "Synthetic" works, instead of analyzing or breaking down the object in the earlier sense, were now precisely and carefully selecting only certain aspects of a given form which could be used to build up or synthesize a new more strongly organized and decorative composition.

Figure 12.
Guitar, Glass, and Bottle
(1912), collage
(paper, newspaper, and felt)
and greyish-blue paper
18¾″ x 24⅝″
Tate Gallery, London

The outbreak of World War I in 1914 dispersed the international circle from Paris. Some of Picasso's closest friends, among them Braque and the critic Apollinaire, went into the armed services; the unique partnership with Braque was never resumed after Braque returned with a head wound. Wilhelm Uhde, a thoughtful writer on Picasso's art and collector of his early work, was forced as a German national to quit France; and Kahnweiler, now Picasso's principal dealer, was likewise deemed an enemy alien. As a neutral foreign subject, Picasso was not required to fight for his adopted France, but the wartime environment forced upon him an unprecedentedly sovereign existence, and deprived of the stimulus of collective scrutiny, the rhythm of his work underwent a change.

His explorations still continued with the invention of the Rococo style of Cubism, so-called because of its tenuous link with the gaiety and minute touch of French eighteenth-century painting (though it is actually closer to the pointillist brushwork and chromatics of Seurat and Signac). The color, vivaciously spotted upon flat, angular shapes which had evolved from the Synthetic collages, became brighter than ever before. His systematic dotting with brilliant hues was extended to sculptures, such as the whimsical bronze sculpture, *Glass of Absinthe* (Slide 11). These three-dimensional or high-relief compositions of the mid-1910's, especially the constructions or assemblages of discarded wood and cardboard shapes, were a strategic contribution by Picasso to early abstract sculpture in both Eastern and Western Europe, although Picasso himself invariably retained an identifiable subject.

At the same time that Picasso pursued such experiments, he astonished his friends by creating a series of superbly realistic pencil portraits of Ambroise Vollard (Figure 13), Max Jacob, and other intimates. The flawless correctness of these likenesses suggests that Picasso was reverting to an earlier mode of expression; but actually the contrary is true. His earlier direct studies from nature, while remarkable for their appeal and linear incisiveness, lack the full discipline and control which years of Cubist study gave to the drawings of 1915 and later. These may, in fact, anticipate the painted works of that sharp-edged phase of Cubism which Maurice Raynal designated "Crystal," such as the 1916 *Guitarist* (Slide 12). No connection between the Vollard drawing and the *Guitarist* is immediately discernible, but close comparison reveals a kindred interpretation of major planes, edges, and verticalization of spatial structure.

Picasso's activities since 1904 had centered in Paris, even though he had visited Holland and revisited Spain and had occasionally worked summers elsewhere in France. Early in 1917, however, he accepted Jean Cocteau's invitation to plan the decor for the ballet *Parade,* which Diaghilev's Ballets Russes was rehearsing in Rome. Picasso's Cubist friends viewed his acceptance as a betrayal of Cubism, still under violent attack from both critics and public. Cocteau wrote of their reaction: "Montmartre and Montparnasse were under a dictatorship. We were going through the puritanical phase of Cubism. Such articles as may be found on a café table together with a Spanish guitar were the only ones allowed. It was treason to paint a stage-setting, especially for the Russian Ballet." *(Picasso,* L. Buchheim, Viking, 1959). However, Picasso's sojourn in Italy and the excitement of involvement with the Ballets Russes,

Figure 13. *Portrait of Ambroise Vollard* (1915), pencil on paper, 18⅜″ x 12½″
Metropolitan Museum of Art, New York, Whittelsey Collection, 1947

which lasted until 1924, strongly affected his life and art. While applying the Cubist aesthetic to stage design and costumes for the *The Three-Cornered Hat, Pulcinella,* and other productions, he became friends with the composers Stravinsky and De Falla, and in 1918 he married the Ballets Russes dancer Olga Koklova.

Picasso's first-hand study of classical archaeology in Rome and elsewhere in Italy was the stimulus for a series of massively structured figures which appeared soon after 1920 (Figure 14 and Slide 13). Concurrently with the development of such powerfully modeled images, Picasso, influenced by his recent experiences in ballet design, exploited the flatly patterned style of early Crystal Period works. The brilliance of that manner, which contrasts with the neoclassical figure style, is demonstrated by *Three Musicians* (Slide 14), a monument of late Crystal Period Cubism which has been called a show window of Picasso's achievements. This sharp-cut, lucidly chromatic mode which Picasso also applied to still lifes (Slide 15) continued simultaneously with monumental figure compositions until 1924.

The advent of the Surrealist movement in 1925 and its widely publicized spread during the late 1920's coincided with Picasso's independent exploration of dreamlike, often grotesque themes. While the Surrealists sought the prestigiousness of Picasso's association, he was never formally a member of the group. They reproduced the works of his so-called Surrealist phase in their official journal, *La Révolution Surréaliste,* and exhibited them with their own; but the slick, overworked manner of the orthodox Surrealists and the self-conscious mystification of their approach could not lastingly appeal to an artist of Picasso's authority. His outstanding canvases from this period are as independent in imagery as in technique (Figure 15, and Slides 16, 17). The *Girl Before a Mirror* especially reveals how Picasso retained the underlying discipline of earlier Cubist methods while projecting a dramatic female allegory of physiological and chronological change.

Sculpture once again claimed Picasso's attention, and since the early 1930's three-dimensional art has commanded much of his energies. In the late 1920's he created a series of remarkable, almost abstract wire and rod constructions which for him were an unprecedented kind of art although they are related to line and dot drawings he had made in 1924 (Figure 16). These openwork pieces were followed by a group of attenuated, icon-like female figures in wood (later cast in bronze); and then came full-volumed bronze heads and animals.

It is not surprising that Picasso has been so interested in sculpture. Even in his Surrealist works, he intrigues us as much by form as by subject. After the early 1930's Picasso's innovations continued to stem from the Cubist base, no matter how arcane his themes. The more severe features of the Analytic style no longer appear, but the basic Cubist approach still remains. The nightmarish iconography of Picasso's great etching, *Minotauromachy,* of 1935 (Figure 17) may be associated with Surrealism, as the raw havoc of the 1937 mural *Guernica* (Figure 18) has sometimes been called Expressionist. But both works belong structurally to Cubism and the remarkable extent to which Picasso continually modifies or accentuates that style is frequently overlooked.

Figure 14.
Three Women at the Spring
(1921)
oil on canvas, 80¼″ x 68½″
Museum of Modern Art
New York
Gift of Mrs. Allan D. Emil

26

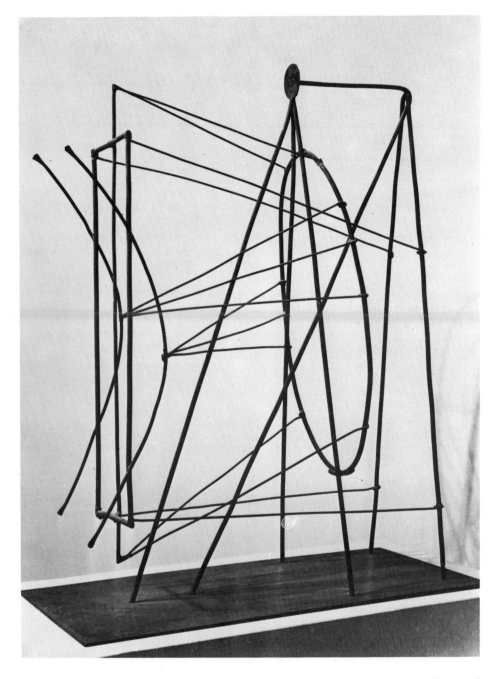

Figure 16.
Construction in Wire (1930)
height 12⅝″
Private Collection

Figure 15.
Girl before a Mirror (1932)
oil on canvas, 63¾″ x 51¼″
Museum of Modern Art, New York
Gift of Mrs. Simon Guggenheim

Figure 17.
Minotauromachy (1935)
etching, 19½" x 27¼"
Museum of Modern Art
New York

Figure 18.
Guernica (1937)
oil on canvas (portable mural)
138″ x 308″
on extended loan to the Museum of Modern Art, New York
from the artist, P. Picasso

The huge mural *Guernica* well illustrates the flexibility of Picasso's Cubism: a theme of extraordinary chaos is unforgettably interpreted by a heroic yet disciplined method. There are no bright tonalities in *Guernica;* its explosive forms are brushed in black and white and a great range of grays—a chromatic restraint which exceeds even that of early and Analytic Cubism.

The mural was commissioned by the official Republican government of Spain in January, 1937, to be exhibited at the forthcoming World's Fair in Paris that June. In late April, a news bulletin about the civil war then raging between the Spanish Republic and fascist forces outraged Picasso and dictated the subject of the mural. Fascist, German-made aircraft unexpectedly bombed the defenseless Basque town of Guernica and machine-gunned the refugees. Slaughter and holocaust were the awful residue.

The symbolism of *Guernica's* haunting images has since been treated in whole volumes; but few interpretations may be made with certainty. Even the significance of the bull as against that of the horse is conjectural. Picasso's own comments amount to the insistence that his mural is a protest not specifically against the fascist aggressor at Guernica (although Picasso, loyal to the Republic, was anti-fascist); nor did this astonishing painting necessarily indict war itself, at least in primary intent. It was rather an outcry against human brutality to other humans, and the horrendous attack on a specific place served as the catalyst. There are not, in fact, enough precise references in *Guernica* to denote that a city has been subjected to military bombardment. The painting at first baffled visitors to the Spanish pavilion at the Paris World's Fair; but the impact of this great protest against bestiality, all the more powerful because of the underlying firmness of the composition, has since deeply reached millions of observers.

Picasso's disturbing personal fortunes during the 1930's almost certainly influenced the choice of the disquieting themes of *Minotauromachy* and *Guernica* as well as many other unforgettable works of this period. Although he was honored by major exhibitions in France and abroad and was now an internationally recognized personality, his personal life had become upsetting. After seventeen years of marriage, he and Olga formally separated in 1935, although the divorce action was never made final because Picasso was not willing to give up his Spanish citizenship. His new companion Marie-Thérèse Walter, who appeared as early as 1932 as the model of *Girl Before a Mirror,* bore him a daughter, Maia, in the year of his parting from Olga. Marie-Thérèse was soon replaced by Dora Maar who remained with him through the next difficult ten years.

The devastations of war in Spain and the rise of Hitlerism also upset Picasso greatly. He traveled more often than usual, visiting Spain for the last time in 1933 and 1934 before the outbreak of the civil war and in 1937 went to see Paul Klee, a fugitive from Nazi oppression, in Switzerland. He also spent intervals at many places in France, among them Cannes, Juan-les-Pins, Le Tremblay-sur-Mauldre, and Mougins, but finally resettled in Paris.

Picasso in 1938 and 1939 became much more productive and was stimulated by living at Antibes on the Riviera, an appealing coastal environment which certain of his biographers have considered to be influential upon his choice of gayer local color and lighting. An important retrospective of his work was presented by the Museum of Modern Art, New York, in 1939; and, despite the ill fortune of the Spanish Republic in the civil war, Picasso became more optimistic than he had been for several years. However, 1940 brought a catastrophe which threatened the light of creativity itself: the invasion of France by the German military forces.

Picasso, the epitome of the avant-garde artist stifled and labelled "degenerate" in Germany and Austria, did not know what lay ahead for him in Paris under Nazi rule. Ironically, the occupation headquarters was located quite near his studio on the Grands-Augustins. But, aside from being forbidden to exhibit his art in public, he was not restricted. Though Nazi officers sometimes intruded out of curiosity, there was no destruction of his work.

Nevertheless, the privations and reprisals of the occupation had their effect on Picasso's moods and productivity. The death of his old friend Max Jacob in a concentration camp was especially saddening. But the analogies often drawn between such conditions and certain of Picasso's subjects and spatial compressions (Slide 18) seem forced. The animal skulls of his wartime still lifes and sculptures had appeared much earlier, and he frequently used them long after France was liberated. The lighted candle in a 1945 composition had been anticipated ten years before in *Minotauromachy* (Figure 17). If claustrophobic symbolism is ascribed to the windowless interiors of certain 1940-1944 compositions, then we must re-examine scores of Picasso's works from each major phase of his development since spatial condensations and tensions lie at the core of his Cubist style.

It is, in fact, the absence of thematic or structural innovation during the years of the Second World War that is the clue to Picasso's state of mind at that time. His masterwork of the period is, interestingly enough, based on a theme which goes back to preclassical antiquity, his over life-sized sculpture *Shepherd Holding a Lamb* (Figure 19). This forceful affirmation of man's humanity was modeled in less than a full day's time in 1945 but was not cast until after the war when bronze once again became available.

Picasso's environment grew unprecedently public during the late 1940's, evidently without great resistance on his part. Joining the French Communist party soon after the liberation of Paris, he was sought out for a time by a stream of political visitors at Vallauris in southern France, where he had moved in 1948. He appeared and spoke at peace congresses in Poland and elsewhere between 1947 and 1951; and in the latter year, at age seventy, he painted *Massacre in Korea.* Picasso made certain concessions to the specific signs of modern warfare, although neither aggressors nor victims are nationally identified; but the Communists found the work insufficiently realistic for propaganda purposes, and critics of style deplored its failure to match the formal power of *Guernica. War* and *Peace,* two huge murals painted in 1952 and installed in an old secularized chapel in Vallauris, which Picasso converted into a Temple of Peace, are more convincing in design than is *Massacre in Korea;* but the effect of the cavorting nudes and threatening warriors is curiously toylike. The posthumous portrait of

Figure 19.
Shepherd Holding a Lamb (1944)
bronze, height 86½"
Philadelphia Museum of Art
Mr. and Mrs. R. Sturgis Ingersoll, reversion

Stalin, which he was reluctantly persuaded to paint by close friends in the French Communist party, was ridiculed by Communists and art critics alike. Picasso's most effective works since World War II have been those in which he was fighting only for greater expressiveness—partisan ideas of other persons and programs have not emerged convincingly in his art.

His productivity since 1948, when he settled with Françoise Gilot in Vallauris, has been incredibly great. He has been strongly creative in the fields of ceramics and lithography. Before Picasso and Mlle. Gilot separated in 1953 and he took Jacqueline Roque as his companion, he restudied the works of several traditional masters and began to create a remarkable sequence of interpretations (Slide 19 and Figure 20). He has brought Poussin, Velázquez, El Greco,

Figure 20.
The Rape of the Sabines (1962)
oil on canvas
38¼″ x 51¼″
Musée National d'Art Moderne
Paris

Delacroix, Courbet, Manet, and other masters into new and brilliant context, translating their great styles in the rich light of his own authority as an old master of recent art.

His *The Rape of the Sabines* (Figure 20) belongs and does not belong to the same milieu. Poussin and David are among those who long ago treated its theme. It has been suggested that Picasso was inspired in this instance by the threat of nuclear war during the Cuban crisis. If this is the case, then Picasso's response was as personal as it had been in *Guernica* twenty-five years earlier; *The Rape of the Sabines* moves us through the great power of style integrated with excitement of theme. Its flavor is not that of the partisan murals of the early 1950's, for the root subject of man's threat to man takes precedence over political propaganda.

Picasso's late years have continued to bring restatements of themes and modes which reach back into the early stages of Cubism (Slide 20). His physical environment, too, is a synthesis of old and new places: Collioure and Paris and Mougins, his huge villa "La Californie" at Golfe-Juan, and Vauvenargues in Provence. Old friends—Kahnweiler, Sabartés, Cocteau—and more recent ones enriched Picasso's intellectual and social milieu.

To how great an extent has Picasso's Spanish origin contributed to the total creative environment in which he continues to work? Certain of his biographers have emphasized the Spanish quality of Picasso's every gesture, as if he will next time surprise us by making a French gesture or a Portuguese or Icelandic one. But it is one thing to say that Picasso is Spanish and another matter to insist that his art is a distinctively Spanish art. It may be true that certain dramatic characteristics of his color or line, of the bravura and contrasts of his design, generally correspond to our romantic notions of Spanish pride, drama, and melancholy. But for each such analogy we may also discover one which relates other facets of his expressiveness to French, Greek, Roman, or primitive origins. Picasso himself has spoken with equal enthusiasm about Velázquez, Cézanne, Rembrandt, Cranach, the ancient Greeks.

Picasso, is, in fact, the first twentieth-century painter whose art is wholly international in its aesthetic basis. It happens to be in part Spanish; but there is much more. In order to discover a new way of painting, Picasso first had to create special conditions of inspiration in all aspects of his personal and professional surroundings. He began to form those conditions in Barcelona in the 1890's; but he has repeatedly changed them as his vision has grown and as he has enhanced our way of seeing. Picasso's environment has been shaped by his own imagination.

COMMENTARY ON THE SLIDES

1: PORTRAIT OF A WOMAN (1901), oil, 20½" x 13"
Rijksmuseum Kröller-Müller, Otterlo

Picasso's drawings and paintings from the first ten months of 1901 reflect his admiration of Toulouse-Lautrec and the Nabi Bonnard as well as of the Impressionists Edouard Manet and Edgar Degas. Critics have called this phase of his development the Cabaret Period, and Picasso himself more than once spoke of the impetus he found in the café and dance-hall subjects of late nineteenth-century French art. But, *Portrait of a Woman* is more than just a reflection of the young Spanish painter's acknowledged influences; it perpetuates and amplifies the female type which he had drawn and painted in Barcelona, and takes its place late in a sequence of studies which show his continuing search for independent expression. He also gives to *Portrait of a Woman* a distinct painterly quality, and he is less dependent than was Lautrec upon the velocity of line and flow of silhouette.

The cascade of brilliant patches of color is not only handsome for its chromatic values, but serves to reinforce and enliven the entire design of this appealing work. The subtle tilting of the head away from the vertical axis enhances the spatial interest. An especially charming element of this small painting is the kinship between the girl's pensiveness and the cool, deeper tonalities beyond the warm hues.

2: THE BLIND MAN'S MEAL (1903), oil, 37½" x 37¼"
Metropolitan Museum of Art, New York
Gift of Mr. and Mrs. Ira Haupt, 1950

Among the many pictures notable for extreme pathos of theme during Picasso's Blue Period, one finds a number of studies of blind persons. Sir Roland Penrose has written of the young Spaniard's preoccupation with the possible loss of his vision, and of his desire to distinguish between merely seeing objects and actually "knowing" them. Though Picasso, in fact, has enjoyed phenomenally excellent sight, his haunting fear of blindness caused him, particularly during the Blue Period, to feel a certain empathy with persons who were sightless or suffered defective vision. The poorer quarters of Barcelona, Madrid, and Paris, with their desolate people and many blind or deformed beggars, offered Picasso innumerable subjects for study (as in the astonishing portrait of the old procuress *Célestine,* whose left eye is blurred by a cast).

It is well known that many people who become blind soon sharpen other faculties of awareness, especially the sense of touch. Picasso seems to share the forlorn anxiety of the blind man in this gripping picture as the fingers nervously search out not only the identity of the meager things beneath them, but also their suitability and lack of threat. Does the bleak universe of *The Blind Man's Meal* simulate the dread void of blindness? Those who might best answer cannot know.

3: LA VIE (1903), oil, 77⅜″ x 50⅞″
Cleveland Museum of Art
Gift of the Hanna Fund, 1945

Before 1903 Picasso had often drawn or painted the motifs of embracing and huddled couples as well as standing mothers with children; but as H. L. C. Jaffé has observed (*Pablo Picasso,* New York, 1964), *La Vie* is an allegorical summary of the artist's view at that time of the tragedy of life. It is also the largest composition of the Blue Period style.

Few of Picasso's Blue Period canvases contain so general an iconography as *La Vie.* There are elements which show withdrawal and tension, especially the strained void between the embracing couple and the woman and child. The sketched images of crouching figures in the background are in cowering or dejected attitudes, and a certain pessimism pervades the imagery. Still, the three principal figures in the foreground are less gaunt and tense than are many of the Blue Period subjects of 1901-1904; and even though the characteristic blue tonality dominates, Picasso assigns extensive passages of pink and warm grays to the undraped forms.

We have been verbally conditioned to perceive only melancholy in paintings which are saturated by blue; but, whatever may be the actual meaning of the allegory of *La Vie,* its gravity results less specifically from the color, in which the warmer notes are important, than from the strange placement and complex facial expressions of its inhabitants.

4: ACROBAT'S FAMILY WITH AN APE (1905)
oil, 41″ x 29½″
Konstmuseum, Göteborg

Picasso's search for unique expression drew him in early 1905 to the environment of circus performers. His excited admiration of their fine sense of timing and professional agility may have helped to warm his colors and to impart a more optimistic psychology than had been present in the Blue Period pictures. Most images of the early Rose Period acrobats, harlequins, and jugglers show the subjects at rest rather than during their tensely skilled performances. *Acrobat's Family* is a masterpiece in its span of contrasting forms, from the wiry figure of the performer at the left, through the less sparse dimensions of the young mother and child, to the squat mass of the ape (actually a species of baboon) at the right. Picasso builds a scale of counterbalances of smallish, dark accents against paler, larger passages; and a kindred variegation occurs in his use of line, blade-thin at the acrobat's upper arms, for example, but dense and shadowy at the ruff of his costume.

Although apes frequently appeared in medieval and Renaissance works where they often had symbolic meaning (Albrecht Dürer's *Virgin and Child with a Monkey,* for example), Picasso's inclusion of the animal here appears to be related to the circus theme rather than to prototypes in older art. The poses of the figures and their proportions are closer to Italian Mannerist counterparts, those of Parmigianino, for example, than to El Greco.

5: THREE DUTCH GIRLS (1905), gouache on paper, 29¾" x 25⅞"
Musée National d'Art Moderne, Paris

A one-month visit to Holland in the summer of 1905 suggested new subjects and tonalities which enriched the scope of Picasso's development in the Rose Period. Blue now becomes a sparkling color which sings in the foreground and middle distance, and echoes in fainter passages of a lavender variant in the sky. Although draftsmanship would continue to be an important aspect of his Rose Period works, Picasso in this Dutch theme shows his growing interest in the value of hue, tone, and volume.

As in other pictures of this and the preceding phase, the artist gave human dignity to the plain subjects he interpreted. The German poet Rainer Maria Rilke wrote an essay on another Rose Period canvas, the renowned *Family of Saltimbanques* (now in the Chester Dale Collection of the National Gallery of Art, Washington); but the *Three Dutch Girls* is, among the 1905 works, almost singularly poetic. It is possible that Renaissance and Baroque interpretations of the "Three Graces" motif lie behind Picasso's rhythmic placement of these unclassical but appealing figures.

6: PORTRAIT OF GERTRUDE STEIN (1906), oil, 39½" x 32"
Metropolitan Museum of Art, New York
Bequest of Gertrude Stein, 1946

Critics still question the extent to which the American writer Gertrude Stein, who knew Picasso intimately during his formative period, actually comprehended the artist's ideas. Nonetheless, Miss Stein, herself a co-seeker of new modes of modern expression, was insistent that radically creative forms were required by a new, quickening century. In any case, she and Picasso talked energetically about that subject during their frequent meetings. (She sat at least eighty times during 1906 for this celebrated portrait and stated that she later came to resemble it.)

Many observers have found Picasso's severe reduction of Miss Stein's face to be "masklike," attributing it to the influence of Iberian classical sculptures which Picasso had seen at the Louvre and in Spain during the summer of 1906. The painting as a whole, however, suggests that Cézanne was a more likely stimulus, for although the bulk of that Post-Impressionist's work was not known to most Parisian artists until the Salons d'Automnes of 1906 and 1907, Picasso had surely seen his paintings in the great collection of the dealer Ambroise Vollard. Gertrude Stein's face, in fact, is less inscrutable than are most of Cézanne's likenesses of his wife and friends; and, far from being masklike, it appears to contain a myriad of attitudes. Especially notable is the contrast between the curiously terse features, which herald a forthcoming modernity in Picasso's style, and the relaxed, beautifully drawn hands, which belong stylistically to the nineteenth century.

7: STILL LIFE (1908), oil, 28¾″ x 25⅞″
Solomon R. Guggenheim Museum, New York

Like Velázquez and other traditional Spanish masters of figure painting, Picasso sometimes turned to the still life; although typically preferring figural subjects, he not infrequently used table arrangements during his early Cubist search for new ways of depicting form. His collaboration with Georges Braque, an ardent admirer of Cézanne, undoubtedly sharpened his appreciation of Cézanne's genius for still life composition as well as calling his attention to the still life as an appropriate subject for prolonged, intensive Cubist analysis.

This 1908 canvas, like certain germinal elements of Cubism itself, relates to the tradition of Cézanne; Picasso establishes each unit of form only after deliberating its relevance to the overall design. But his execution is swifter than Cézanne's, the spatial intervals more staccato, the definitions of silhouette sharper. There is an imposing sweep of cool and neutrally toned shapes and of passages from the lower foreground toward the upper left sector of the composition; and the subtly positioned vase of warm terra cotta forces the eye to span the interval from left to right. Picasso's vertical structuring of objects anticipates the more emphatically upright, flatly conceived paintings of Analytic and later Cubism in the second decade of the twentieth century. It should be noted that Picasso modifies the effect of his spatial innovations and distortions of form by limiting his palette to restrained grays, green-blues and greens, and earth colors.

8: WOMAN IN GREEN (1909), oil, 37¾″ x 31½″
Stedelijk Van Abbemuseum, Eindhoven

The seated figure was a prominent theme in Picasso's 1909-1911 development of Cubist style. *Woman in Green* is characteristic of a remarkable series of studies and portraits in which, with bold reduction of the particulars of natural appearance, the artist brought early Cubism to what is known as the Analytic phase.

This canvas, painted during the winter of 1909, belongs to both periods. Its color sustains the tonal notes of the 1908 *Still Life* (Slide 7) as well as certain Spanish landscapes of the following year, but with deeper shades of green; and the space now becomes shallower, the form more severely reduced and fragmented as in the 1910 Analytic works. Picasso all but eliminates the conventional middle ground of space as the strong image of the woman thrusts upward and, with the back of the chair, almost merges with the plane of the wall. He is intensely concerned with the essentials of form and features, suppressing local detail and emphasizing solids, planes, angles, convexities. He has not, however, abandoned his subject, but, rather, has subordinated her specific, identifiable features in favor of a penetrating analysis of form.

We are not certain of the sitter's name; but she, like Fernande, Clovis Sagot, Braque, and others who posed for Picasso during this period, undoubtedly sat time and time again before the painter felt that he had grasped the formal essence of her image.

9: THE ACCORDIONIST (1910), oil, 51¼″ x 35⅛″
Solomon R. Guggenheim Museum, New York

Cubism deemphasizes and restructures the specifics of objects, but rarely is the basic representation of the subject completely abandoned. Even during the summer of 1911 when Picasso and Braque joined Cubist analysis of form with the concept of simultaneity, wherein the front, sides, and even parts of the back of a form are revealed all at the same time, the actual subject of the painting never appeared completely abstract. Then, as always, Picasso's style combined conceptual and visual qualities. Analytic Cubism faceted and dissected solids and planes, but reassembled them into a systematic context, no matter how unfamiliar. We see the accordionist in a new and more complex state of visual reality. Dr. Robert Rosenblum, an especially thoughtful historian of Cubism, has compared the deliberately altered identities of such subjects as this one with the multiple roles of Joyce's Leopold Bloom of *Ulysses* who was at once businessman, Greek hero, Jesus, Hamlet.

The recorded statements of both Picasso and Braque show their intense concern with the total relevance of their subjects rather than with the founding of a conceptual system of art as such. It is doubtful if the realists Caravaggio and Courbet ever more searchingly studied their models; and, no matter if we discover the figure of the accordionist only after following a complex of cryptic signs, the subject remains primary to the total effect of this Cubist masterpiece.

10: BOTTLE, GLASS, AND VIOLIN (1912/13)
papier collé and charcoal, 18½" x 24⅝"
Nationalmuseum, Stockholm

Students of the Synthetic style of Cubism once held that Picasso's and Braque's use of clipped paper shapes, imitation wood-graining, bits of musical scores and newspapers, and other unconventional materials was a satirical introduction of "real" substances into painting after critics assailed the "lack of realism" in Cubist compositions. It is more likely that during the winter of 1911-1912, Picasso and Braque began to feel that most possibilities of the severe Analytic manner had been exploited and that *papier collé* or collage offered exciting new challenges for spatial and textural exploration. Even in the austere method of Analytic Cubism, Picasso's brushwork had clearly revealed that his planes and arcs had issued from a painterly touch. But a certain magical quality results from the substituting of unconventional substances for painted areas; and in many Synthetic Cubist collages, an empty cigarette package, a playing card, or a musical score was affixed to the surface literally to represent itself—hence, a synthesis in reverse, so to speak, with reality replacing the traditional painted image.

A new clarity of shape and greater openness of design appears in such works as *Bottle, Glass, and Violin,* yet Picasso to some degree modifies the sharpness of the cut-out patterns by drawing around and upon them in the soft and conventional medium of charcoal.

11: THE GLASS OF ABSINTHE (1914)
painted bronze and silver spoon, height 8¾"
Philadelphia Museum of Art, A. E. Gallatin Collection

The idea of combining different media in one sculpture did not originate in the twentieth century but was widely practiced in ancient art and during the Middle Ages and the Renaissance; gold and ivory, wood and iron, bronze and silver were often combined, and many classical and Gothic statues were brightly painted. The Italian Futurist Boccioni was probably the first modern sculptor to advocate the use of bizarre, anti-traditional substances in serious art, although Picasso and the Russian Constructivists were evidently the first to actually use unorthodox materials in this way.

The Glass of Absinthe, cast by Picasso from a real absinthe glass and perforated spoon as well as a real lump of sugar, is a parody not only on the sculptural media, but upon itself.

The bronze glass cannot possibly be used as a drinking vessel, for it is ventilated along one side; and its gay spottings of pure color, which are typical of Picasso's painted works of the so-called Rococo phase, are deliberately irrelevant to the sculptural form. Works of this kind are related to the "ready-mades" of Marcel Duchamp, who, like Picasso, anticipated the whimsical character of Dada art (officially founded in 1916) and Pop creations of the 1950's and later.

12: GUITARIST (1916), oil, 51" x 38"
Nationalmuseum, Stockholm

Since most of his colleagues in the Cubist movement were scattered by the advent of World War I, Picasso, a neutral alien residing in France, had to pursue Cubist aims without the advantage of accustomed discussion and study of his friends' researches. The *Guitarist* belongs to this period of Cubism (called the Crystal style) which extended to paintings from late 1915 until the mid 1920's, even though Picasso also worked simultaneously with other approaches.

The canvases of the Crystal-style manner are even more strongly vertical in composition than those of the Analytic Period in which this tendency had already developed. Small accents of chromatic spotting carry over from the Rococo style of 1914-1915, and serve as a textural foil to the sharp-edged, flat trapezoids and rectangles which dominate this towering design. The upper and lower zones are dramatically locked in space by the dovetailing of sharp-cut dark forms into lighter shapes and the effect of tightly mortised joints which results. Picasso again uses as his subject the musician who had appeared in both the Blue and Analytic Periods, thus retaining an earlier theme as well as key formal elements of previous styles.

13: MOTHER AND CHILD (1921), oil, 65½" x 64"
Art Institute of Chicago

The years during and immediately following World War I brought many changes to Picasso's life and painting. From 1917 until 1924 he created designs for the Ballets Russes of Sergei Diaghilev, and in 1918 married one of the ballerinas, Olga Koklova. Cubism now found its place in the brilliant decor of modern dance.

The year 1921 found Picasso painting in two major styles—Crystal Cubism and a classical manner—and several lesser ones, all of them to some degree based upon his own previous explorations. *Mother and Child,* whose primary theme often appeared in his very early art, belongs to a sequence of massively formed figures, some of them nude and others draped in chiton-like robes. Many are shown near sources of water, especially the sea or a fountain.

Picasso's 1917 visit to Italy, occasioned by his connection with the Russian Ballet, was the immediate stimulus for these subjects. Some of them, such as pipe-playing youths, have specific prototypes in ancient Greek and Roman sculpture or vase painting. But no Hellenic figures equal the gigantic scale of Picasso's so-called neoclassical women. The more massive proportions of certain late Roman carvings are a likelier source; and Picasso himself in 1906 had anticipated, with a few powerfully modeled female nudes, this remarkable aesthetic of the early 1920's. *Mother and Child* is a major example of the sculpturesque tradition of Picasso's art.

14: THREE MUSICIANS (1921), oil, 80″ x 74″
Philadelphia Museum of Art, A. E. Gallatin Collection

Two huge canvases on this theme resulted from Picasso's stay at Fontainebleau during the summer of 1921. (The second, slightly larger version, in which a dog is added, is in the Museum of Modern Art, New York.) Both paintings are monuments not only of late or Crystal Cubism but of twentieth-century art.

Three Musicians is remarkable not only for its great scale and resonant color, but for its opposition of major and minor light and dark shapes, its provocative calligraphy, and the curiously intermingled solemnity and gaiety of the overall imagery. Equally magnetic are its extra-visual denotations, particularly those which suggest sound—not only the musical instruments and score but Picasso's syncopation of shapes and tones—as well as those suggesting touch sensation such as the gently overlapping shoulder planes. The flatly formed figures are beautifully keyed to one another, almost as if slotted and bracketed by the series of pale blue verticals, yet each musician has a clear identity. A fourth head is formed in profile—almost punlike— at the juncture of the central figure's hands upon his woodwind. It has become all but a ritual to discern in Picasso's art a peculiarly Spanish flavor; but the provocative intervals and tensions of *Three Musicians* are more nearly parallel with Austrian, German, and Russian atonal innovations than with either traditional or modern Spanish music.

15: MANDOLIN AND GUITAR (1924), oil, 51½″ x 56″
Solomon R. Guggenheim Museum, New York

This boldly patterned composition relates to other still lifes of 1921-1923 and to earlier paintings in the Crystal style, but its span of colors and diversity of shapes are unusually striking. Picasso also amplifies the spatial treatment common to other works, enlarging the box-like void of the composition and defining it with short orthogonal lines in the floor, windows, and shadows. He has also opened the central zone of the wall upon a balcony and a clear blue sky with a triad of white clouds. Both the blue and the white are echoed in the interior scheme, establishing a complex but certain optical path. The spectator may at once perceive the total design of *Mandolin and Guitar,* multiple though its components may be.

Few artists of any period in the history of art have been able to impart to the still life the sense of drama which Picasso brings to this and another vivid arrangement of 1924, *Still Life with a Black Head.* These and similar canvases both extend the mode of preceding works and point toward more liberated, even frenzied compositions such as the renowned *Three Dancers* of 1925 (Tate Gallery, London).

16:   BATHER PLAYING WITH A BALL (1932), oil, 57½″ x 44⅞″
Mr. and Mrs. Victor W. Ganz Collection, New York

Some of Picasso's most imaginative works, from *The Poor at the Seaside* of 1903 to the 1921 *Mother and Child* (Slide 13) and quite recent paintings, have been concerned with beaches and bathers. Between 1927 and the early 1930's, he created a remarkable series of monster-like figures by the sea—some of them drawn or painted to resemble openwork constructions of bones, others shown with distorted foreshortening or perspectival emphases. Many of these disclose the artist's acquaintance with the Surrealist movement.

Bather Playing with a Ball is structured with such buoyant forms that we wonder if Picasso was not engaging in one of his visual-verbal puns, in this instance involving the word "bouncy." The volumetric shapes are rubbery, bounding; and their rhythmic interplay dominates the composition. The shading of the rounded surfaces is distantly related to the more programmatic—and often slick—modeling characteristic of much surrealistic art of this period; but, although Picasso associated with certain of the Surrealists and exhibited with them as early as 1925, his style and dreamlike iconography of the early 1930's were unique. Picasso was familiar with both sex and circular or spherical painterly motifs long before the Surrealists somewhat belatedly discovered Freud.

17:   SEATED WOMAN WITH A BOOK (1937), oil, 51¼″ x 38⅛″
Private Collection

From his early student days until the present Picasso has enjoyed the phenomenal ability to depict natural appearances or to transform them. His most rewarding works have resulted from his need to create a special anatomy which transcends the normal way of seeing. This drive led first to Cubism and then to a number of astonishing drawings and canvases of 1929 which have been called "bone period" works. Again in 1937 he produced a series of pictures whose forms, like those of the so-called bone period, are warped and pulled into a grotesque, sometimes inhuman framework.

Seated Woman with a Book suggests the presence of a dream-image creature whose simplified skeleton has somehow become externalized, then again clothed in its own skin, and finally inflated. In spite of this ordeal the woman, whose tiny eyes seem incapable of function, languidly studies an indecipherable page. Works of this weird, independent order explain why the Surrealists at this time gladly claimed Picasso as an unofficial contributor to their program; but, unlike many widely publicized Surrealists, even Picasso's most bizarre themes are paralleled by an equally original manner of expression. The true force of paintings like *Seated Woman with a Book* is Picasso's relentless search for style.

18:   L'AUBADE (also known as *Nude with a Musician*) (1942)
oil, 76¾″ x 104½″
Musée National d'Art Moderne, Paris

Two of Picasso's favorite artists, Jean Dominique Ingres and Henri Rousseau, were among those who used the theme of sleeping or reclining women being serenaded. *Aubade* means "morning song" in French, but the recumbent female in this angular composition looks remarkably sleepless. She is wide-eyed, and her brittle, striped bedding and the slab-like couch are hardly conducive to notions of rest. The mandolinist, like the distended figure, is a woman. She does not play the instrument but appears to have been thwarted from beginning her jingling melody of the early hour. The scene offers no figment of romance or comfort.

Some writers see an analogy between the cramped, windowless interiors of such wartime canvases as *L'Aubade* and the horrors of compressed torture chambers or cells in concentration camps. There can be no question of Picasso's personal revulsion at the Nazi occupation of Paris and all it entailed, even though he himself was not victimized nor seriously restricted. But his paintings of 1940-1944 were clearly anticipated in both theme and manner by earlier works, and, far from discarding such developments after the liberation of France, he continued for some years to occasionally use compact space, skulls, and other motifs of the World War II compositions. *L'Aubade* is the largest canvas he produced during that period.

19:   THE WOMEN OF ALGIERS (1955), oil, 40 7/16″ x 57½″
Mr. and Mrs. Victor W. Ganz Collection, New York

Picasso has long admired Eugène Delacroix, the great nineteenth-century romantic innovator, not only for his pictorial genius but for the insurgent spirit with which he attacked the restrictions of the official academy of his day. This painting is one of more than a dozen versions directly inspired by Delacroix's 1834 canvas *Women of Algiers*.

Picasso's version of the painting is a firmly if complexly counterbalanced structure of vivid contrasts of hue and shape and texture. There is more than an overtone of the 1910-1914

Cubist tradition in his reduction of the broad plan of Delacroix's work to related angular and semi-circular planes; and the sharp value oppositions of both large and small shapes reminds us of the strongly vertical patterns of canvases from the late 1910's. The striped and hatched elements of *The Women of Algiers* recall counterparts in the *Mandolin and Guitar* of 1924 (Slide 15) and *Girl Before a Mirror* of 1932 (Figure 15). Jacqueline Roque, who in 1954 became Picasso's companion and subsequently his wife, was probably the model for the imposing figure at the left.

20: WOMAN'S PROFILE ON RED BACKGROUND (1959)
oil, 31¾" x 25½"
Collection of Dr. Kurt Forberg, St. Moritz

Women seated in chairs have long been favored subjects in Picasso's art. This theme became especially prominent during the 1930's and again in the early 1950's when the model Sylvette sat for the "ponytail" series. Jacqueline Roque, at first identified as "Madame Z" in a 1954 study, then succeeded as principal sitter in a sequence of paintings called "Women in the Studio."

Woman's Profile on Red Background is at once appealing and forceful. The face may be seen in both profile and three-quarters view, an arrangement which long since had become recognized as characteristic of the Cubist concept of simultaneity. The half figure is sharply projected against a flat red surface whose strident color is held in place by the jagged, clear flesh tone which breaks through it and carries tiny accents—the fingernails—of identical red. Another color, black, is applied as flatly and vividly as are the other tones; the chromatic effect of this black, assigned to the provocative shape of the coiffure, is closely related to the fourth color, the cool green of the dress. The thin linear lines of the chair form a contrast to the broad patterns of the woman's figure.

RECOMMENDED BOOKS FOR MORE DETAIL

Barr, Alfred H., *Picasso: Fifty Years of His Art*. New York: Museum of Modern Art, 1946. An outstanding study, well-illustrated, of Picasso's stylistic development.

Boeck, Wilhelm, and Jaime Sabartés, *Picasso*. New York: Harry N. Abrams, 1955. A thoughtful interpretation of the artist's themes and major styles. Sabartés, a lifelong friend of Picasso, provides biographical notes.

Hommage à Pablo Picasso. Paris: Grand Palais and Petit Palais, 1966-1967. An excellent catalog of a monumental exhibition of the artist's painting, sculpture, graphic work, and ceramics. Copiously illustrated.

Penrose, Sir Roland, *Picasso: His Life and Work*. London: Gallancz, 1958 (and New York: Schocken, 1962). A detailed biographical work which also examines Picasso's entire growth as an artist.

Raynal, Maurice, *Picasso*. Geneva: Editions Albert Skira, 1953. Handsomely illustrated; written by one of the early enthusiasts of Cubism and a friend of Picasso from 1904.

Zervos, Christian. Various articles and an extensive, well-illustrated catalog, in *Editions Cahiers d'Art*. Vols. I-XII, Paris, 1932-1961.